A Teen's Coaching Tool Towards Embracing *Equity and Diversity*

By Christine Gibson, Ph.D.

with

Christina L. Lee & Yvette I. Hall, MBA

Paradigm 360° Publishing, LLC

Charlotte, North Carolina

Copyright © 2021 by Paradigm 360° Consulting

All Rights Reserved.

Published by Paradigm 360° Publishing, LLC

9611 Brookdale Drive, Suite 100-252, Charlotte, NC 28215

No part of this publication may be reproduced, stored in a retrieval system, or transmitted in any form or by any means, electronic, mechanical, photocopying, recording, or otherwise, without the prior written permission of publisher.

www.paradigm360consulting.com

info@p360coach.com

ISBN: 978-0-578-24413-6

Instructional Designer: Dr. Christine Gibson

Guide Graphic Designer: Aaron J. Ratzlaff

Cover Designer: Tobi Idowu, Spgdesign

Dedication

This book is dedicated to School Superintendent Cheryl Turner and the wonderful administrators at Sugar Creek Charter School. It has been an honor to serve the administration, faculty, and students over the last several years. Thank you for modeling leadership, integrity, and authenticity in the lives of more than 1,700 students daily. Sugar Creek Charter School is a staple in the Charlotte community serving as one of the oldest charter schools in our city's history. Your commitment to education is unprecedented and second to none.

We would like to give an honorable mention to the Late Mrs. Mildred Jackson Sadler, a trailblazer and trendsetter in education who served as Gaston County Schools' first African American administrator in the field of Human Resources. Mrs. Sadler ultimately paved the way for her son, the Late Dr. Edward D. Sadler, Jr. who served as Gaston County's first African American Superintendent of Schools. Both of these educators broke racial barriers, stereotypes, and fostered a movement of equality in executive leadership within the world of education. Thank you, Mrs. Mildred Jackson Sadler and Dr. Edward DeWitt Sadler, Jr. Your labor of love for education and leadership has opened the doors for many people of color, and for that, we give you honor, may your legacy live in the lives, hearts, and careers of educators for years to come.

To my (Christina Lee) personal mentor of more than 40 years Bonnie Hill, Ed.D., who served three presidential appointments under the leadership of President Ronald Regan and President George H.W. Bush, Sr., she has also served on a dozen Fortune 500 corporate boards and was the first woman and African American to serve as lead director for The Home Depot Corporation. Bonnie Hill and her highly distinguished, pioneering business partner and husband Walter Hill (Retired CEO of Icon Blue) have shattered the glass ceiling leaving room for countless people of color to soar in the world of free enterprise. Thank you, Bonnie and Walter, for modeling excellence, leadership, and business integrity.

Acknowledgments

We would like to formally thank the following individuals – without your help and support this project would not have been possible.

To our spouses and children. Thank you for allowing us to champion our dreams often at your expense due to the long hours we put into building the lives and leadership potential of others. We are indebted to your deep levels of sacrifice that allow us to carry out our calling and purpose. We love each one of you from the depth of our hearts.

To the Paradigm 360º staff, board of directors, coaches, and supporters. Thank you for allowing space for vision, innovation, and collaboration, as we work toward "Building World-Class Leaders One Conversation at A Time" Your labor of love for this organization has been tremendous.

To the Paradigm 360º Young Entrepreneurs. It's our hope that this book will continue to add value to the countless conversations we've had regarding your future as marketplace leaders. Your future goals and ambitions continue to provide wind beneath our wings. Thank you for creating a space for us to serve as leaders in your young lives.

To our core team of Summit Conference speakers: Executive Coach Nate Salley, Coach David "Dae-Lee" Arrington, Coach Charles "DJ Sir Charles" Sledge, and Life Coach Erika Shorty. Thank you so much for believing in the vision of Paradigm 360º and the Young Entrepreneurs program. We wouldn't have tremendous success without your dedication and commitment to our vision to serve young people across the Charlotte region. Thank you and we are honored to call you Paradigm 360º Coaches.

To my (Christina Lee) two daughters Shannon and Danielle who are both educators. I hope the pages of this book will make you proud. Yvette and I can't begin to tell you how proud we are to see you both flourish in your gift as educators. Please use this book as a tool to have transformational conversations throughout your tenure in education.

To Harrison Hunter, my co-host on the Young Entrepreneurs Podcast. Your wisdom, dedication, and an entrepreneurial mindset are beyond your years. Your mom (Yvette Hall) and I are super proud of how you have conducted yourself as a leader amongst many. Your future endeavors are countless.

To Mrs. Tawana Wiggins, principal of Sugar Creek Charter School, (J Frank Martin High School Campus). Thank you, for trusting Yvette and me with over 300 youth that are entrusted to your leadership. Your dedication and loyalty to education have been a joy to glean from. You are a fantastic educator.

To Ms. Vicky Merritt thank you, for your loyal friendship and continued support of Paradigm 360º. You are an educator among educators, your unfailing love and dedication for the middle and high school students you've served over the years as principal is nothing short of amazing. Thank you for the paradigm shift you've made in the lives of many.

To Dr. Melissa Balknight, Associate Superintendent of Schools, Gaston County. Thank you for the opportunity to serve the wonderful educators and students in Gaston County Public Schools. Your leadership is creating a wonderful pathway and future for the more than 30,000 students in your district. Thank you for all you do.

A Note to Facilitators

Thank you for investing in your youth by purchasing *"A Teen's Coaching Tool Towards Embracing Equity & Diversity"* This workbook was designed to facilitate student-led transformative conversations. In a non-traditional teaching environment, students will have opportunities to explore life-changing self-awareness through collaboration with their peers and adult leaders on the topics of Diversity, Equity, and Inclusion.

The case studies were designed with fictional characters in real-world situations. *"A Teen's Coaching Tool Towards Embracing Equity & Diversity"* was birthed out of the racial unrest experienced in the year 2020 during a world pandemic. In many ways, efforts have been made to deal with the inequities many have experienced in life. However, we believe that there is still much to do in the areas of Diversity, Equity, and Inclusion. The events of 2020 reiterated the need and desire for humanity to come to the table and engage in much needed authentic conversation so we can bridge the gap through powerful dialogue. We hope you enjoy these conversations as much as we did when putting this body of work together.

Lastly, this content is designed to help students engage in authentic conversation responsibly around topics that some may consider sensitive. Therefore, the authors and publisher are not responsible for any actions taken by facilitators or readers engaged in the study.

Next Stop Transformational Relationships!

A Teen's Coaching Tool Towards Embracing Equity and Diversity

This curriculum introduces a balanced approach to building relationships cross-culturally and across socioeconomic boundaries.

Paradigm 360º Teen's Coaching Tool Towards Embracing Equity and Diversity is a great instrument to support a balanced approach to building relationships cross-culturally and across socioeconomic boundaries. The five pillars of Social and Emotional Wellness outlined in this tool are designed to deliver best results when used in a setting where dialogue is welcomed and collaboration is encouraged. You may use this guide independently as well as in a collaborative learning setting (i.e., in a home or classroom environment). Please see the following website for an optional facilitator guide. https://paradigm360consulting.com/facilitator-resources-for-teen-diversity-book.

Objectives

- The student demonstrates their understanding of the five pillars of Paradigm 360º.
- The student will recognize how Social and Emotional Learning intersects with Social Justice, Political Views, Socioeconomic classes, Bias thinking, and Diversity.
- The student will identify Conscious and Unconscious Bias and its impacts both positive and negative.
- The student will recognize the importance of their identities.
- The student will recognize the impact of their voice.
- The student will demonstrate ways to dismantle obstacles and challenges.
- The student will understand the value of having a balanced perspective.
- The student will create ways to make a positive impact in their homes, schools, and communities.

Table of Contents

Dedication 3

Acknowledgments 4

A Note to Facilitators 6

Objectives 7

Foreword 9

Chapter 1-a. Becoming Aware of Self 11
    Vocabulary 15

Chapter 1-b. Becoming Aware of our Biases 16
    Case Study 18
    Case Study (optional) 19
    Activity 22
    Vocabulary 23

Chapter 2. Building Sustainable Communities 24
    Activity 28
    Vocabulary 29

Chapter 3. Practicing Self-Governance 30
    Case Study 33
    Vocabulary 34

Chapter 4. Making Accountable Choices 35
    Case Study 38
    Vocabulary 39

Chapter 5. Fostering Authentic Relationships 40
    Activity 43
    Vocabulary 44

Privilege Points 45

Glossary 48

References 51

Wrap Up Activity 53

About the authors 59

Foreword

Honor defined: *Honor is a relational or social term that identifies how people in any society evaluate one another's worth. To intentionally honor means to grant respect, value, importance, and relevance to our lives. The key is to honor from the inside-out, i.e., honor who someone is before honoring what someone does.*

I have heard it said that a person's dreams and goals can be swallowed up by the culture around them. Sometimes our gatherings in our homes, neighborhoods, schools, and even shopping malls can reinforce negative aspects of culture that can cause us to give up our personal hopes, become like the people who mistreated us, or even pressure others to not try and be or do anything different than what has always been the norms in those cultures. That seems to be especially true when it comes to the breakdown in healthy diverse relationships that our culture seems to be reinforcing around us.

I know a solution. I call it creating a culture of honor. It can be seen in families, schools, businesses, neighborhoods, and even prisons when there are people dedicated to training and empowering others to honor themselves, their conversations, and the relationships they will develop. When those people are coaches then the dishonor in any culture is on the run!

Paradigm 360 is one of my favorite group of coaches that are shifting cultures in difficult places. I am so thrilled to see their amazing track record already of transforming teens and their cultures. Now they are focused on this training, giving teens a coaching tool for diverse relationships that are healthy and honoring. These coaches know how to honor… and are passionate about bringing that skill to the young people who will not be smothered by the culture they face.

Several years ago these wonderful Paradigm 360 culture changers were in my inaugural workshop called "I Brand Inside". We showed 12 video clips of 12–17- year-olds who were making a difference now, not someday when they grew up. Many of them did it in spite of the cultural negatives they faced in their communities. The 75 youth and youth workers in that room discovered that day that this very age group could become the key to the culture change we must have. This phrase from the workshop seemed to capture what happened:

> *"I'm not defined by the clothes I wear or the people around me or by anything external. I am defined by me: by who I am and by who I am becoming. I am unique. I am designed to make a difference. I was meant to make waves. I am destined to be a world-changer. I am*

empowered to defend the powerless. No person is outside my borders, my circles of honor, or my ability to forgive. I am not small enough to create walls. Everyone is my brother, my sister. We are one!"

We reap what we sow but we reap later than we sow, and we reap more than we sow. I believe the content of this Diverse Relationship workbook and the character of these coaches is the fulfillment of what was sown in this "I Brand Inside" event years ago. I am amazed to see how much more teens will receive because of the heart of honor that will be created through this experience. I am humbled to know that many of these empowered teens will stand on my and the Paradigm 360 coaches' shoulders and impact culture one diverse relationship and honoring conversation at a time.

Grateful,

Dr. Joseph Umidi
CEO/Founder Lifeforming Leadership Coaching
EVP Regent University

Chapter 1-a. Becoming Aware of Self

How does my identity, thoughts, and actions fit into the spaces I have been placed in society? Understanding who you are and the power you possess is essential. Social and Emotional Wellness supports how we, as humans understand:

1. Who we are
2. Why we make individual choices
3. Our connection with others
4. How we self-discipline
5. And how we thrive in different social environments

According to Paradigm 360º, social and emotional wellness can be achieved through five pillars, which they believe will unlock sustainable changes in applying a balanced approach to building relationships cross-culturally and across socioeconomic boundaries. Let's begin with becoming self-aware.

Paradigm 360º defines becoming self-aware as the ability to manage one's interpersonal communication skills while building bridges with others without feeling the need to change one's value systems. Our consciousness is the seat of our emotions and thought processes. What we believe controls our decisions and how we behave. Sometimes, we may find that we don't know what we don't know because of our lack of experience in certain areas.

Becoming Self-Aware may support:

- Appreciation of differences
- Positive self-image
- Realization of potential
- Self-efficacy
- Self-reflection

Merriam-Webster defines **Self-Awareness** as an awareness of one's own personality or individuality.

Positive Psychology defines **Self-Awareness** as the ability to see yourself clearly and objectively through reflection and introspection.

As individuals, we embark on a journey to understand ourselves, all while considering our environment. Who are your influencers? To what extent do these individuals and groups play a role in defining one's self and the perceptions of others? Your perception and ideas of self may determine how you weigh in on political, religious, educational, sexual, ethical, cultural views, and more. And how you view yourself also influences how you view others.

The culture in which we emerged or grew up, our experiences, and lack of experiences mold us into the individuals we are. These are all factors we need to consider when defining ourselves. Again, how we view ourselves plays a significant part in how we view others. Our lived experiences, and the experiences of individuals close to us play a huge factor in how we perceive ourselves, our political views, how we see individuals in differing social and economic classes, and the degree to which we accept others of diverse backgrounds.

 A Paradigm Moment

- What or whom are you using as a measure to define who you are?
- What group(s) is your identity tied to? Explain.
- Who are the individuals close to you that your identity is tied to?
- Are you defining yourself by what you were taught at home? How well do you follow your home culture expectations?

One important thing to consider when thinking about becoming more self-aware as it relates to change is: **Why do you matter?**

Understanding the value of you and your own identity supports understanding the importance of the identities of others. Drawing from Dr. Bettina L. Love's beautifully written novel titled, *We Want To Do More Than Survive: Abolitionist Teaching and the Pursuit of Educational Freedom* gives a deeper meaning to why we as individuals must matter.

"I learned above all else to protect my dignity. My dignity was never to be compromised, which meant never compromising my voice and my connection to how I mattered in this world. When you compromise your voice, you compromise your dignity. No dignity, no power. Knowing I had a voice backed by common sense, which I understood was supposed to be used to protect myself, was one of the most powerful things I have ever been taught."

Dr. Bettina L. Love

Your voice is a powerful tool when it comes to breaking barriers. Understanding the weight of your voice may create endless possibilities for change.

Why is it important to understand the factors that influence you as an individual?

_____

_____

_____

Do you have the same expectations for others as you do for yourself? Explain your answer.

_____

_____

_____

How does self-awareness play a part in your political, religious, educational, sexual, ethical, and cultural views? Explain.

_____

_____

_____

Do you believe that your voice has power? Why or why not?

_____

_____

_____

How can you use your voice for change?

_____

_____

_____

Is it possible for one person's identity to threaten another person's rights? Explain.

_____

_____

_____

Vocabulary

WORD	DEFINITION

Chapter 1-b. Becoming Aware of our Biases

When thinking about becoming self-aware, it is essential to consider one's personal biases. Let's define bias and examine different types of partialities.

Bias

Psychology Today defines **bias** as a tendency, inclination, or prejudice toward or against something or someone.

The University of California, San Francisco Office of Diversity and Outreach defines **bias** as a prejudice in favor of or against one thing, person, or group compared with another, usually in a way that's considered unfair. Biases may be held by an individual, group, or institution and can be negative or positive.

Unconscious Bias (Implicit Bias)

According to OSU Kirwan Institute for the Study of Race and Ethnicity, **implicit bias** refers to the attitudes or stereotypes that affect our understanding, actions, and decisions in an unconscious manner.

Stanford Encyclopedia of Philosophy Research on **"implicit bias"** suggests that people can act based on prejudice and stereotypes without intending to do so.

Conscious Bias (Explicit Bias)

According to Georgetown University National Center for Cultural Competence, the **conscious bias** in its extreme is characterized by overt negative behavior that can be expressed through physical and verbal harassment or through more subtle means such as exclusion.

These biases may derive from one's upbringing by way of generations that may have been biased towards certain ethnic groups for different reasons. These beliefs have been imprinted upon one's subconscious or often considered a part of an individual's deep culture. Such inclinations may manifest in stereotypical thinking or ideas that cause one to uphold unfair thought processes subconsciously. Constant self-reflection and willingness to be open to others' realities and being aware that biases exist may help build a better you.

We must remember biases are typical, and we all have them. However, we must acknowledge our biases and be open to alternate narratives as individuals. These conversations may not always align with what you may have been taught or may go against your family norms. Nonetheless, these conversations are vital to understanding others' perspectives. Becoming self-aware plays a critical role in understanding how you think and why these biased thoughts exist.

Case Study

Paradigm High School, located in a predominantly affluent community, is known for high academics, high standards, and strong athletics. After school, Erin and Jeremiah were watching their brother Sam and his best friend Harrison workout on the football field. Sam was the school's All American football star. While watching, Erin's friends Camryn, Morgan, and Mackenzi spotted a young African American boy named Isaiah walking across the field preparing for tryouts. Isaiah was 16 years old 6'4" and 205lbs. The kids heard that he was a recent transfer from Eastside High School clear across town. Sam's friend Harrison pointed out Isaiah and began to whisper, "I think you just lost your position. You're done for!" Sam shoved his curly blond hair out of his face to get a better look at the new kid and thought to himself, "You might be right!" Shortly after, Camryn whispered to Erin, "How did he get to this school?" Erin shrugged her shoulders and said, "I don't know but he sure is cute."

Get in a group or with a partner and unpack this case study.

What biases could be at play in this case study? What are your assumptions about Isaiah? What are your assumptions about Sam? What does Harrison's comment suggest about Isaiah? What does Sam's comment suggest? What can you draw from Camryn's comment to Erin? What are some things the teens did not consider while discussing Isaiah? Did Erin's comment display any biases?

_____

_____

_____

_____

_____

_____

_____

_____

_____

Case Study (optional)

Shannon and Danielle Lee are Asian American twin sisters, and they've attended Paradigm High School since ninth grade. Shannon is outgoing and energetic. Danielle is quiet, shy, and stays to herself; both girls can often be found in the library studying at different times during the day. While both girls work very hard to achieve good grades, many don't know that they struggle academically, especially in Math. However, their hard work is paying off, and they have begun to get offers at local colleges. Shannon has aspirations to major in film, and Danielle would like to be a kindergarten teacher. Kent Wesley, a senior, has had classes with the sisters since ninth grade but has never taken the time to get to know either of them on a personal level. Kent is having some academic challenges that may cost him his rugby scholarship. His teacher Dr. Hall shares several students' names he may want to make contact with for tutoring. After leaving Dr. Hall's class, Kent sees the twins going into Mrs. Lee's Algebra II class and says to himself, "Forget Dr. Hall's suggestions. I'm going to ask Shannon or Danielle Lee to help me because all Asians are smart." "I bet they are going to be doctors or engineers when they grow up." After this private discussion with himself, he yells across the hall to get the girls' attention, "Hey Shannon and Danielle, can I talk to you after the third period?"

Reflect with a group or partner and discuss some of the biases in this case study. What are some of the biases surrounding the twins Shannon and Danielle Lee? What are some of the biases surrounding Kent Wesley? If you were Kent Wesley's close friend, what might you say to him about his comment?

_____

_____

_____

_____

_____

_____

_____

What are some stereotypes about other people or races you have been exposed to?

_____
_____
_____
_____

Is it possible for one person's identity to threaten another person's rights? Explain.

_____
_____
_____
_____

What are some things you can do as an individual to disrupt stereotypes?

_____
_____
_____
_____

How do stereotypes impact you as an individual, and how you perceive others that are unlike you?

_____
_____
_____
_____
_____

Is it possible for your school to be free of biases?

_____

_____

_____

_____

When have your biases stopped you from creating relationships with others unlike you?

_____

_____

_____

_____

Activity

Design a flyer that is thought-provoking that will support eliminating stereotypes and advocating for Equity.

Becoming aware of one's self is a lifetime commitment. Self-reflection is necessary for individuals to begin to challenge their thinking and thought processes. Being able to be empathetic and vulnerable creates pathways to learning. This leads us to the next pillar, Building Sustainable Communities.

Vocabulary

WORD	DEFINITION

Chapter 2. Building Sustainable Communities

Paradigm 360º defines **Building Sustainable Communities** as the ability and willingness to engage in transformational conversations that uncover diverse perspectives.

Building Sustainable Communities may help support:

- Inclusivity
- Empathy
- Vulnerability
- Respect for the inherent value of others

Understanding yourself and how you come to particular views or decisions on many diverse areas of life can be a tremendous support when considering the idea of inclusion of individuals and groups from diverse backgrounds. But first, let's define diversity. Diversity helps break barriers and disrupt inequitable systems. Diversity can offer an alternate perspective of one's thought process. Diversity also creates a space of respect for others' race, gender, age, culture, religion, and so forth.

Merriam-Webster defines **diversity** as the condition of having or being composed of differing elements: *especially*: the inclusion of different types of people (such as people of different races or cultures) in a group or organization.

Dictionary.com defines **diversity** as the inclusion of individuals representing more than one national origin, color, religion, socioeconomic stratum, sexual orientation, etc.

According to Diversity Social, there are four types of diversity dimensions: **internal, external, organizational,** and **world view** (Chan, 2020).

Examples of **internal** diversity are race, age, ethnicity, gender, sexual orientation and appearance, physical ability (to name a few).

Examples of **external** diversity are individual and group interest, education, geographic location, family status, spiritual/religion, socioeconomic status, experiences (to name a few).

Examples of **organizational** are school location, job title, job location, affiliations with a group, and many others.

Examples of **world view** are cultural events, politics, history knowledge, background knowledge, historical accuracy, etc.

Becoming a productive member of society calls for understanding the importance of diversity. It also means being willing to embrace people and situations that you are not familiar with. Some things people do will also go against what you have been taught. The willingness to accept individuals' political views, religious beliefs, and situations can be challenging. However, to have a balanced cross-cultural perspective, one must be willing to take time to empathize with others to gain a broader perspective of the world.

Social Justice

According to Dictionary.com **social justice** is defined as fair treatment of all people in a society, including respect for the rights of minorities and equitable distribution of resources among members of a community.

If social justice is defined as fair treatment to all, one can assume that social injustices are the unfair treatment of society members.

According to the Merriam-Webster dictionary, **injustice** is defined as the absence of justice: violation of right or the rights of another and unfairness.

Being socially aware and building sustainable communities may support you in understanding how and why injustices exist. Embracing diverse individuals and groups begins with the acceptance of others' differences. This makes it possible to empathize and understand the social and ethical norms of others. Individuals must realize that the difference that is needed to make change starts with their personal choices. Are your perceptions of others unlike you, positive or negative? How can different groups work together for everyone's benefit?

Now that we have explored social justice and injustices let's use what we now know and discuss.

 A Paradigm Moment

- How can building sustainable communities bridge the gap when individual's socioeconomic statuses are different?
- How does embracing diversity help you to be socially aware?
- How can empathy be used to better understand the impact cultural norms may cause amongst socioeconomic classes?
- Why do you feel compassion for others when they are mistreated?
- How can different groups work together for everyone's benefit?

Building a sustainable community may support the disruption of social injustices. Understanding that people come from different cultures and backgrounds and have different ethical norms is key to being a part of the much-needed change in this world. People are mistreated because of their ethnic background, sexual orientation, religious beliefs, socioeconomic status, skin color, and political views. People may also be mistreated because of simple things such as the neighborhood they live in, schools they attend, parents, and so much more.

What are some social injustices that you may have been exposed to or noticed?

_____

_____

_____

_____

_____

Why should people that live below the poverty guidelines demand the same respect as those who do not?

_____

_____

_____

_____

When people's beliefs or actions do not match yours, do you respect their differences? Give an example.

_____

_____

_____

_____

How can the lived experiences of individuals reflect social inequities?

_____

_____

_____

_____

What are some privileges that certain groups experience based on their identities and social status?

_____

_____

_____

_____

Activity

Create a campaign that supports building sustainable communities for your classroom or school building that calls for Equity. Make sure it is inclusive of individuals and groups that are not similar to yours. Include persons and groups that may support your campaign. You may also create a vision board that showcases your goal(s) for building sustainable communities. Be sure to include your goal on your vision board with visuals and words representing your purpose.

Vocabulary

WORD	DEFINITION

Chapter 3. Practicing Self-Governance

Self-Governance is a key component to managing one's self. Paradigm 360º defines practicing self-governance as the ability to make a paradigm shift to redirect automatic reactions while assessing one's thoughts and behaviors.

Practicing Self-Governance may support the following:

- Self-Control
- Exercising discipline
- Communication
- Healthy socialization
- Making connections
- Recognizing biases
- Achieving goals/self-leadership
- Resilience

Merriam-Webster defines **self-management** as finding the self-control and mastery needed to take control of one's work.

According to Dictionary.com, **self-management** is the management of or by oneself; the taking of responsibility for one's own behavior and well-being.

Let's discuss the importance of regulating one's emotions and the significance of effectively managing one's self. Controlling your feelings, thoughts, and behaviors can be extremely challenging but also necessary. When faced with an adverse situation or a situation that is unlike anything you may have encountered, it is crucial to control your emotions. Self-governance is key to maintaining and building a healthier, more effective you. Self-discipline also helps to develop and maintain healthy relationships with others.

Practicing self-governance also looks at how individuals manage their thoughts and control their impulses in the presence of people that do not share the same values and norms. One critical factor of practicing self-governance is that individuals must be okay with being uncomfortable. Managing your discomfort level with things that are unfamiliar to you is part of self-regulation. Linking feelings, values, and thoughts by being self-aware and having a deep understanding of your triggers to find balance are also key.

A Paradigm Moment

- What happens when individuals or groups in positions of power do not practice self-governance?
- How does not practicing self-governance hinder your decision making?
- Is it possible to be an effective individual without practicing self-governance skills? Explain.
- When your political, religious, educational, and cultural views are opposed to others, how do you handle yourself?

Practicing Self-Governance is being able to normalize uncomfortable conversations. Fighting for things you believe in is more effective when you can have difficult conversations without making rash, impulsive decisions. People who fight for social justice on various issues must stay grounded and control their impulses when faced with demanding situations. It also helps motivate you as an individual to stay focused on your goals.

A big part of restoring justice for all is practicing self-discipline. Being able to self-regulate and discipline oneself is critical to bridging the gap between socioeconomic classes, cultural differences, and so much more. It also helps to reduce incidences of bullying. Studies have shown that bullying is extremely harmful to one's psychological and physical well-being.

How well do you manage your emotions?

_____

_____

_____

_____

Why is it important to disagree with someone without being overly emotional and making impulsive decisions?

_____

_____

_____

Name three positive outcomes of practicing self-discipline.

    1.

    2.

    3.

Name three possible negative outcomes of not using self-management skills.

    1.

    2.

    3.

Case Study

Imagine you are a school leader in a community that is considered disadvantaged or poor, and your students do not have all the resources needed to be academically successful. However, you value all your students and parents. You find yourself very angry often about the inequitable allocation of resources. How would you approach your employer regarding this matter? Your boss constantly brags about the school buildings within the district in affluent neighborhoods that have an abundance of resources. Remember, your goal is to be effective and get the resources necessary to support your students and families.

Vocabulary

WORD	DEFINITION

Chapter 4. Making Accountable Choices

Paradigm 360º defines **Making Accountable Choices** as practicing self-accountability in making decisions that may affect others.

Making Accountable Choices may support the following:

- Making a positive impact
- Taking ownership
- Being a change agent
- Problem-solving

An excerpt from an article from Today, titled **12th grade responsible decision-making skills**, provides a broader understanding of the importance of relationship skills.

> *"Responsible Decision-Making goal is to build capacity in your school community and in the individuals who comprise that community. It is also taking into account your wishes and the wishes of others. The ability to understand yourself, your actions, how your actions affect others, and what is socially acceptable goes into the responsible decision-making process."*
>
> Jamie Farnsworth Finn

Making Accountable Choices is being aware of the choices you make as an individual and their impact on others. Making Accountable Choices also supports the consideration of others when making decisions. It is essential to self evaluate when making decisions. This may consist of individuals exploring patterns within their choices. Let's examine this concept of patterns as it relates to decision making. Why do I make the same choices repeatedly? Are my decisions always comfortable for me? These are questions to consider when looking for patterns of decision making. Sometimes decisions are made because individuals feel a sense of safety within their choices (physically safe and psychologically safe). However, what is considered safe for one person may not be safe for others.

Self-evaluation and self-reflection are critical as we examine the importance of making accountable choices. One must also consider ethical responsibility when making decisions and identify possible challenges within their choices. Something to also consider is how do your experiences or your upbringing affect your choices?

 A Paradigm Moment

- What rights do you have?
- Do all people have the same rights? Explain.
- How is my life easier or more difficult, based on who I am and where I was born?
- When something is unfair, does it affect everyone the same way? Explain.

Making Accountable Choices places accountability on an individual or group for their actions and choices. Bridging the gap between justice and injustice by taking a stance against inequities progresses humanity forward. As mentioned before, evaluating your biases may help when deliberating on choices that may impact others adversely. Accepting that problems may exist that you may not be aware of is also a huge consideration when making decisions.

Taking ownership of your personal choices is a key component of making accountable choices. Schools are the largest social institution for children and teenagers. Within the school building, you may find various social issues and an array of ideas on dealing with these problems. Issues in a school may arise from biased texts, curricula that are not accurate, community political views, cultural norms, differing ethical standards, and much more. If these issues are not handled responsibly, it may cause a population of students to be isolated or may cause trauma. The goal is to build a capacity in our schools and communities for the people who comprise those groups to make accountable choices.

How would your school be affected if no one chose to stand up to others?

_____

_____

_____

What are some ways your decisions affect others around you?

___

What are some patterns in the decisions you make often? Why do you make these decisions?

___

How do your privileges, or lack of, impact your decisions?

___

Describe a time when you have been impacted negatively by someone else's choices?

___

When should you consider others before making decisions?

___

Case Study

Charles Russell is a transferring student from Paradigm High School from a small town in California. You don't know Charles personally, but acquaintances at Paradigm High have shared with you that Charles is a high achiever, outgoing, and loves to have fun in extracurricular activities. However, you've noticed that Charles has been withdrawn over the past couple of days. Not only has Charles been dismissive, but he has also missed several classes over the last couple of weeks. During Friday night football, some of your closest friends in your circle made unfavorable remarks about him. Over the last couple of weeks, you have been working on being more accountable in relationships and demonstrating your awareness in areas that lack inclusion. Provide an example of how you would openly express accountability and support Charles in this instance. In your explanation, choose either gender, disability, race, sexual identity, or socioeconomic status, causing Charles to isolate himself. Your choice for Charles may also be an area of inclusion that you are working towards.

Vocabulary

WORD	DEFINITION

Chapter 5. Fostering Authentic Relationships

Paradigm 360º defines **Fostering Authentic Relationships** as the ability to share one's truth while simultaneously building bridges and community with others while honoring others' authentic selves. Fostering Authentic Relationships creates spaces for transparency.

Fostering Authentic Relationships may be supported by the following:

- Transparency
- Dialogue
- Creating community
- Building relationship capital
- Equity

According to Definition.net, **Relationships Skills** is the ability, skills, trust, tools, knowledge, knowing, and understanding to create, communicate, evolve, grow, and maintain a relationship

Now that we have explored definitions of Fostering Authentic Relationships let's discuss further. What does it take to build and maintain healthy relationships? By now, you most likely have a better understanding of how all the four pillars mentioned in previous chapters intersect with each other. A key component of building positive relationships is gaining a broader sense of one's self.

When building relationships, it is vital to consider the biases housed within an individual's conscious and subconscious and how they affect one's decisions. This all plays a huge role in building relationships. Many factors play into why individuals may not be able to maintain or build healthy relationships. Some of these factors are differences in race, opposing political views, cultural differences, religious differences, differing norms, sexual preferences, and many others.

Socioeconomic classes may also hinder individuals from building relationships. Historically there has always been a gap between individuals considered wealthy and those that are considered poor. The socioeconomic class that falls in the middle (middle class), gaps exist there as well. The social pressure of remaining with those who share similar statuses may become a barrier to building relationships. Your privilege or lack of it often becomes a critical component when it comes to making healthy relationships.

According to the American Psychological Association, **socioeconomic status** is the social standing or class of an individual or group. It is often measured as a combination of education, income, and occupation. Examinations of socioeconomic status often reveal inequities in access to resources, plus issues related to privilege, power, and control.

Dictionary.com defines **socioeconomic status** as the position or standing of a person or group in society as determined by a combination of social and economic factors that affect access to education and other resources crucial to an individual's upward mobility.

According to Dictionary.com, **privilege** is a special advantage or right possessed by an individual or group. A privilege is a right or advantage gained by birth, social position, effort, or concession. It can have either legal or personal implications.

Far too often, this is how an individual's value is measured and often determines whether or not a relationship will be formed. Sometimes one's privilege may cause division amongst others. When individuals feel that they have higher or more exclusive rights than those who do not share the same privileges, it creates a more comprehensive gap within social groups and society.

 A Paradigm Moment

- How do power and privilege change the way you present yourself when building relationships?
- How does your worldview affect your relationships?
- Why should you be willing to build relationships with individuals that may not share the same values?
- Why is it important to cooperate with others that offer an opposing view to your own?

Fostering Authentic Relationships are critical to all facets of life. Having the ability to establish and maintain healthy relationships, communicate effectively, resolve conflicts, resist peer pressure, and collaborate are essential in all human interaction. These skills are fundamental to success in school and life.

Correspondingly, there must also be Equity within a relationship for it to thrive. Celebrating difference and understanding that difference is what makes everyone unique is critical. Creating spaces where being vulnerable is accepted, and individuals' identities and cultures are welcomed.

Why is it important to check your biases when building relationships?

_____

_____

_____

When considering differing socioeconomic classes, what are some barriers between classes that may hinder individuals or groups from forming relationships?

_____

_____

_____

Describe what Equity in a relationship should look like.

_____

_____

_____

How do power and privilege affect individuals when building relationships?

_____

_____

_____

Activity

Create a one minute and thirty-second commercial that discusses the importance of building positive relationships. Your commercial must include terms such as socioeconomic status, Equity, unity, differing cultures, healthy relationships (these are just a few examples). Be creative and thoughtful of others.

_____

_____

_____

_____

_____

_____

_____

Vocabulary

WORD	DEFINITION

Privilege Points

Activity: Add/subtract points based on the statements.

Many people with certain privileges never notice them because they are so intertwined into the mainstream that those who have them cannot see them. For you, understanding and acknowledging privileges is key to understanding why and how you react and perceive your surroundings. The objective of this activity is to discuss privileges in a reflective manner (Peace Learner, 2016).

Procedures:

- Everyone starts with no points
- Do not add or subtract points unless the statement pertains to you. If it does not, just keep going.
- Add points up at the end and compare results.
- Discuss results and statements that really stuck out to you by using the debrief questions.

1. If you are right-handed, add a point.
2. If English is your first language, add a point.
3. If one or both of your parents have a college degree, add a point.
4. If you can find Band-Aids at mainstream stores designed to blend in with or match your skin tone, add a point.
5. If you rely, or have relied, primarily on public transportation, on, subtract a point.
6. If you have attended schools with people you felt were like yourself, add a point.
7. If you constantly feel unsafe walking alone at night, subtract a point.
8. If your household employs help, such as housekeepers or gardeners, add a point.
9. If you are able to move through the world without fear of sexual assault, add a point.
10. If you studied the culture of your ancestors in elementary school, add a point.

11. If you were ever made fun of or bullied for something you could not change or was beyond your control, subtract a point.
12. If your family has ever left your homeland or entered another country not of your own free will, subtract a point.
13. If you would never think twice about calling the police when trouble occurs, add a point.
14. If your household owns a computer, add a point
15. If you have ever been able to play a significant role in a project or activity because of a talent you gained previously, add a point.
16. If you can show affection for your romantic partner in public without fear of ridicule or violence, add a point.
17. If you ever had to skip a meal or were hungry because there was not enough money to buy food, subtract a point.
18. If you feel respected for your academic performance, add a point.
19. If you have a physically visible disability, subtract a point.
20. If you have an invisible illness or disability, subtract a point.
21. If you were ever discouraged from an activity because of race, class, ethnicity, gender, disability, or sexual orientation, subtract a point.
22. If you ever tried to change your appearance, mannerisms, or behavior to fit in more, subtract a point.
23. If you have ever been profiled by someone else using stereotypes, subtract a point.
24. If you feel good about how your identities are portrayed by the media, add a point.
25. If you were ever accepted for something you applied to because of your association with a friend or family member, add a point.
26. If your family has health insurance, add a point.
27. If you have ever been spoken over because you could not articulate your thoughts fast enough, subtract a point.
28. If someone has ever spoken for you when you did not want them to do so, subtract a point.
29. If there was ever substance abuse in your household, subtract a point.

30. If you come from a single-parent household, subtract a point.
31. If you live in an area with crime and drug activity, subtract a point.
32. If someone in your household suffered or suffers from mental illness, subtract a point.
33. If you have been a victim of sexual harassment, subtract a point.
34. If you were ever uncomfortable about a joke related to your race, religion, ethnicity, gender, disability, or sexual orientation but felt unsafe to confront the situation, subtract a point.
35. If you are never asked to speak on behalf of a group of people who share an identity with you, add a point.
36. If you can make mistakes and not have people attribute your behavior to flaws in your racial or gender group, add a point.
37. If you always assumed you would go to college, add a point.
38. If you have more than fifty books in your household, add a point.
39. If your parents told you that you could be anything you wanted to be, add a point.

Debrief Questions:

- What were some factors that you have never thought of before?
- What question made you think most? If you could add a question, what would it be?
- What do you wish people knew about one of the identities, situations, or disadvantages that caused you to lose points?
- How can your understanding of your privileges, or lack of, improve your existing relationships with yourself and others?

Glossary

Diversity - Merriam-Webster defines diversity as the condition of having or being composed of differing elements: *especially*: the inclusion of different types of people (such as people of different races or cultures) in a group or organization.

Diversity - Dictionary.com defines diversity as the inclusion of individuals representing more than one national origin, color, religion, socioeconomic stratum, sexual orientation, etc.

Bias - Psychology Today defines bias as a tendency, inclination, or prejudice toward or against something or someone.

Implicit Bias - According to OSU Kirwan Institute for the Study of Race and Ethnicity implicit bias refers to the attitudes or stereotypes that affect our understanding, actions, and decisions in an unconscious manner.

Implicit Bias - Stanford Encyclopedia of Philosophy Research on "implicit bias" suggests that people can act on the basis of prejudice and stereotypes without intending to do so.

Relationship Skills - the ability, skills, trust, tools, knowledge, knowing, and understanding to create, communicate, evolve, grow, and maintain a relationship.

Social and Emotional Learning (SEL) - Social and Emotional Learning as the process through which children and adults acquire and effectively apply the knowledge, attitudes, and skills necessary to understand and manage emotions, set and achieve positive goals, feel and show empathy for others, establish and maintain positive relationships, and make responsible decisions.

Becoming Self-Aware - the ability to manage one's interpersonal communication skills while building bridges with others without feeling the need to change one's value systems.

Building Sustainable Communities - the ability and willingness to engage in transformational conversations that uncover diverse perspectives.

Practicing Self-Governance - as one's ability to make a paradigm shift to redirect automatic reactions while assessing one's thoughts and behaviors.

Making Accountable Choices - as practicing self-accountability in making decisions that affect others.

Fostering Authentic Relationships - the ability to share one's truth while simultaneously building bridges and community with others while honoring others' authentic selves.

Unconscious Bias (Implicit Bias) - According to OSU Kirwan Institute for the Study of Race and Ethnicity, implicit bias refers to the attitudes or stereotypes that affect our understanding, actions, and decisions in an unconscious manner.

Stanford Encyclopedia of Philosophy Research on **implicit bias -** people can act based on prejudice and stereotypes without intending to do so.

Conscious Bias (Explicit Bias) - According to Georgetown University National Center for Cultural Competence, conscious bias, in its extreme, is characterized by overt negative behavior that can be expressed through physical and verbal harassment or through more subtle means such as exclusion.

Socioeconomic Status - According to the American Psychological Association Socioeconomic status is the social standing or class of an individual or group. It is often measured as a combination of education, income, and occupation. Examinations of socioeconomic status often reveal inequities in access to resources, plus issues related to privilege, power and control.

Dictionary.com defines **socioeconomic status** as the position or standing of a person or group in society as determined by a combination of social and economic factors that affect access to education and other resources crucial to an individual's upward mobility.

Bully - a blustering, mean, or predatory person who, from a perceived position of relative power, intimidates, abuses, harasses, or coerces people, especially those considered unlikely to defend themselves.

Bullying - According to StopBullying.gov bullying is unwanted, aggressive behavior among school aged children that involves a real or perceived power imbalance. The behavior is repeated, or has the potential to be repeated, over time. Both kids who are bullied and who bully others may have serious, lasting problems.

Affluence - the state of having a lot of money or owning many things.

Affluent - having an abundance of goods or riches.

Poverty - the state of one who lacks a usual or socially acceptable amount of money or material possessions.

Social Justice - Dictionary.com defines it as fair treatment of all people in a society, including respect for the rights of minorities and equitable distribution of resources among members of a community.

Injustice - the absence of justice : violation of right or of the rights of another and unfairness.

Disadvantage - Merriam-Webster defines it as lacking in the basic resources or conditions (such as standard housing, medical and educational facilities, and civil rights) believed to be necessary for an equal position in society.

Disparity - Vocabulary.com defines it as a difference that is unfair: economic disparities exist among ethnic groups; there is a disparity between what men and women earn in the same job.

Privilege - Dictionary.com defines it as a special advantage or right possessed by an individual or group. A privilege is a right or advantage gained by birth, social position, effort, or concession. It can have either legal or personal sanction: *the privilege of paying half fare; the privilege of calling whenever one wishes.*

References

Abolitionist Teaching Network (2020). Guide for Racial Justice & Abolitionist Social and Emotional Learning. Retrieved from: https://abolitionistteachingnetwork.org/guide

Affluence, Retrieved from: https://dictionary.cambridge.org/us/dictionary/english/affluence

Affluent, Retrieved from: https://www.merriam-webster.com/dictionary/affluent

American Psychology Association. (2020). Socioeconomic status. Retrieved from: https://www.apa.org/topics/socioeconomic-status

Bullying, Stop Bullying.gov., Retrieved from: https://www.stopbullying.gov/bullying/what-is-bullying

CASEL (2020). Social Emotional Learning. Retrieved from: https://casel.org/what-is-sel/

Chann, B. (2020). Diversity Social. Retrieved from. https://diversity.social/workplace-diversity-types/

Dictionary.com. (2020). Privilege. Retrieved from: https://www.dictionary.com/browse/privilege

Dictionary.com. (2020). Socioeconomic status. Retrieved from: https://www.dictionary.com/browse/socioeconomic-status

Disadvantage, Retrieved from: https://www.merriam-webster.com/dictionary/disadvantaged

Disparity, Retrieved from: https://www.vocabulary.com/dictionary/disparity

Finn, J.F., (2020). 12th grade responsible decision-making skills. Today Retrieved from: https://www.today.com/parenting-guides/12th-grade-responsible-decision-making-skills-t178983

Kirwan Institute for the Study of Race and Ethnicity (2020). OSU. Retrieved from: https://kirwaninstitute.osu.edu/

Layne, R., & Chiu, R. (2016). Privilege walk lesson plan. Presentation, Carter School for Peace and Conflict resolution, George Mason University, Fairfax, Virginia. Retrieved (Dec., 2020)

Love, L. B. (2019). We want to do more than survive : abolitionist teaching and the pursuit of educational freedom. Boston/ USA: Beacon Press.

Positive Psychology. (2020). Self-Awareness. Retrieved from: https://positivepsychology.com/self-awareness-matters-how-you-can-be-more-self-aware/

Poverty, Retrieved from: https://www.merriam-webster.com/dictionary/poverty

Privilege, Retrieved from: https://www.dictionary.com/browse/privilege

Psychology Today.(2020). Bias. Retrieved from: https://www.psychologytoday.com/us/basics/bias

Racial and Equity (2020). Retrieved from: https://www.racialequityinstitute.com/groundwaterapproach

Relationship Skills, Retrieved from: https://www.definitions.net/definition/relationship+skills#:~:text=Editors%20Contribution-,relationship%20skills,and%20evolve%20with%20each%20other.

San Francisco Office of Diversity and Outreach. (2020) bias. Retrieved from: https://diversity.ucsf.edu/resources/unconscious-bias

Self-Awareness, Retrieved from: https://www.merriam-webster.com/dictionary/self-awareness

Self-Management Retrieved from: https://www.merriam-webster.com/dictionary/self-management

Wrap Up Activity

Spend some time thinking about each of the five pillars and develop a **S.M.A.R.T** goal for the areas in which you believe you need the most growth. The acronym **S.M.A.R.T** stands for the following:

S – Stands for **Specific**: You can state clearly what you want to accomplish

M – Stands for **Measurable**: You've included a way to measure your results

A – Stands for **Attainable**: It's within your capabilities and depends on you alone

R – Stands for **Relevant**: The goal is a personal priority

T – Stands for **Time-Specific**: It has a deadline

Sample **S.M.A.R.T.** goals may sound like the following:

"I would like to learn how to turn my B in science to an A by the end of the next semester."

"By the end of the summer, I would like to meet one friend who does not live in my neighborhood and is of a different ethnicity."

Develop your **S.M.A.R.T.** goal around **Becoming Aware of Self**

Develop your **S.M.A.R.T.** goal around **Building Sustainable Communities**

Develop your **S.M.A.R.T.** goal around **Practicing Self-Governance**

Develop your **S.M.A.R.T.** goal around **Making Accountable Choices**

Develop your **S.M.A.R.T.** goal around **Fostering Authentic Relationships**

About the authors

Dr. Christine Gibson is an educator and an innovative thinker. Dr. Gibson has a passion for instructing children and adults and improving the education process through specialized curricula and individualized instruction. Dr. Gibson has led numerous professional development training to support educational professionals and to enhance their classroom practices. She received her Associate's Degree in Early Childhood Education while she worked as a Head Start teacher for fourteen years. Advancing her education while working as a Lead Teacher, Dr. Christine Gibson obtained her Bachelor's Degree in Liberal Studies from Northern Kentucky University. Dr. Gibson then went on to acquire her Master's Degree in Multicultural Special Education from Mount St. Joseph University. She began her career as an Education Coach, where she assessed educators inside the classroom to ensure best practices were being administered. Dr. Christine Gibson then became an Intervention Specialist for Cincinnati Public Schools while earning her Doctorate in Early Childhood Education on February 14, 2020. Dr. Christine Gibson currently serves as the English Language Arts Curriculum Council Chair for the district.

Dr. Christine Gibson is also the founder and CEO of Continuous Growth Educational Services LLC and has partnered with Dream Builders University as their Executive Director of Curriculum and Instruction. She enjoys writing children's books and curriculum to support healthy development for children and adults alike. Dr. Gibson also serves as a member of the NAACP Education Committee Cincinnati Chapter. She also serves on the board for Black Parent Magazine and holds a certification as a Paradigm 360º coach.

Christina Lee is the Chief Executive Officer for Paradigm 360º Coach Training, LLC. She has a wealth of experience in corporate, non-profit management, fundraising, and development. Prior to leaving corporate America she served as District Director for Junior Achievement of the Bay Area and was responsible for supporting the organization in its annual 3.5-million-dollar operating budget through corporate and individual giving and managed a district advisory board of C-Suite Executives. She's also skilled in building teams through behavioral management assessment-based trainings, developing over 4500 leaders within a ten-year span. Since 2004 she has successfully trained small companies, school districts, and non-profit organizations. She holds a certification as an Executive Leadership Coach from Dream Releaser Coaching, A Coach Trainer Certification from Life Forming Leadership Coaching, MBTI Certification, and Disc Certification. She is a Prosci Change Management practitioner, a Lean Six Sigma Green Belt, and certified Diversity Equity and Inclusion practitioner. Christina is a native of Oakland, California, has a wonderful husband of more than thirty-four years and six adult children. She's a national speaker, teacher, executive coach, and serves as Assistant Chaplain to NFL families through the Professional Football Players Mothers Association, chaplain for her local police department, and serves as an EOA board member for one of the world's largest Entrepreneurial Organization (EO). One of her greatest joys in life is her involvement with the Paradigm 360º Young Entrepreneurs program, a program that develops and prepares young talent for future marketplace leadership. In her spare time, she enjoys reading, podcasting, and vacationing on California beaches.

Yvette I. Hall, MBA is the Co-Founder and Chief Operating Officer of Paradigm 360º Coach Training, LLC. She holds a Bachelor of Arts in Political Science from UCLA and an MBA in Marketing and General Management from The Stephen A. Ross School of Business at The University of Michigan. Yvette also holds a certification as Executive Life Coach from Dream Releaser Coaching and Coach Trainer Certification from Lifeforming Leadership Coaching. She is a Prosci Change Management practitioner, a Lean Six Sigma Green Belt, and a certified Diversity Equity and Inclusion practitioner. She has had a successful 20-year career in marketing, sales, and business development, working in senior management for several Fortune 100 companies. She taught at the collegiate level for nearly ten years at Johnson C. Smith University where she also served as Department Chair for the Business and Economics Department for several years. She loves teaching and developing young people. Yvette is a native of California. She and her wonderful husband currently reside in Charlotte, North Carolina with their two college-age sons and two dogs. In her spare time, she enjoys family time, travel and she is finishing up her Ph.D. in Marketing at Hampton University.

www.ingramcontent.com/pod-product-compliance
Lightning Source LLC
Chambersburg PA
CBHW040055160426
43192CB00002B/78